Melton Constable
Briston and District

*A Further Portrait
in Old Picture Postcards*

Rhoda Bunn

JOHN NICKALLS PUBLICATIONS

This book is dedicated to daughter Chrissie and grandson Tony,
who always come up smiling no matter what Fate throws their way

BY THE SAME AUTHOR
Holt and District
Melton Constable, Briston and District, Book One

ISBN 1 904136 13 3

Front cover: Briston Road, Melton Constable

First published in 2003 by John Nickalls Publications,
Oak Farm Bungalow, Sawyers Lane, Suton,
Wymondham, Norfolk NR18 9SH

Designed by Ashley Gray and Printed by Geo. R. Reeve Ltd.,
9–11 Town Green, Wymondham, Norfolk NR18 0BD

Contents

Foreword

WHAT a joy! How fortunate we are having such a rich heritage of photographs and postcards. Seeing all these old pictures of Briston, Melton Constable and the surrounding villages has brought back so many memories.

I was born at 13 The Lanes, Briston in 1941 and went to the local school at the age of five, with some of my first memories being taken to school on the first day by my mum and being in what seemed like a large class, with a huge coal fire, and a bottle of warm milk mid-morning. One of the highlights of those early days I recall being the Funfair on the school green each year.

My parents owned one of the local shops selling anything and everything. But they were long days with the shop being open from 6am to 8pm. A half-day on Wednesdays gave time for a trip into Norwich to buy more goods.

Briston at that time was quite a sleepy village, we had the playing fields and pavilion and the Oddfellows' Hall. This was used for many functions; whist drives, dances, weddings and parties, but best of all as a cinema on Thursdays, Fridays and Saturdays – the same film all three nights, mostly cowboys. We used to pay sixpence in old money to sit in the front row.

There were many shops, five pubs and fish and chips from Mr Godfrey's shop – very hot and eaten out of the paper. The horse-drawn milk cart, the coal cart and sometimes the 'honey cart' were seen in the villages. There was also a man on a bicycle with a large basket on the front selling cockles and shellfish.

At fifteen-years-of-age I started playing football and cricket for Briston, going round all the villages and sometimes sharing the field with cows and sheep. Briston also used to hold an inter-village cricket tournament; Woodfield, Hall Street, West End and Mid-Village. This was always played with great enthusiasm.

After leaving school I went to Norwich Art School. This meant an early morning cycle ride to Melton Constable Station and then a Steam Train journey to Norwich City Station, stopping at lots of the villages on the way.

My training now completed, I am now a full-time watercolour artist and living in Sheringham, but still travelling and painting around the same small villages of my childhood.

It has been a great pleasure writing this foreword and reading this book has brought back such lovely memories.

Martin Sexton
Sheringham

Introduction

SINCE *Melton Constable, Briston and District* came out in 1991 I have had so many letters from folks pleased to find pictures of themselves, or their forebears in it, that I thought, in this book, a further portrait of Melton Constable and District, I would add extra pictures of groups and individuals. My first book was such a success that it sold out in a matter of weeks and it had been difficult to get it reprinted owing to the former publisher's ill-health, but then along came John Nickalls and reprinted it and has now published the second volume, not before time I might add, as I have just celebrated my 79th birthday!

As I gave short summaries of both Melton and Briston in my first book, I thought the subject of town and village photographers would suffice in this introduction, as it is thanks to them that there are a great many pictures in this book.

Many towns had photographers, eg Caves of Dereham, May Bone of Fakenham and, of course, Preston Bros of Holt.

Mr H Remington was Briston's photographer. He could be seen pushing his bicycle round with the camera tripod strapped to the crossbar en route to take pictures at some destination. He recorded many village happenings, Flower Shows, Sports Days and the like, and also those in surrounding villages. He also did portraits at his house in the Lanes which had diamond-patterned panes in the windows. His portraits were taken against the background of these windows and were easily identifiable.

He was a multi-talented man, being a very good painter in oils. There is an excellent picture of Briston Fair at night in existence, signed by him. He also played the violin and gave piano lessons. One of his pupils, Miss Elsie LeGrys would accompany him on the piano, while he played the violin at concerts in the Oddfellows' Hall.

Today, most people have their own cameras and only visit town photographers for weddings or portraits, so the little village photographers have all but died out.

Melton Constable has changed considerably since the closure of the Railway and Briston seems to have grown a great deal, with many houses being built, but fortunately some things remain the same as I remember them.

I hope readers of this book will enjoy it as much as my first book. It has certainly been a pleasure for me to put it together.

Rhoda M Bunn
49 Market Street, Wymondham
October 2003

Abbreviations: c. – circa ***p.u.*** – postally used

PUBLICITY FOR MELTON BOOK ONE – 1991

Mr Michael Rutland sold many of the *Melton Constable, Briston and District* books in the Butchers' shop in Melton Main Street. The picture shows Mrs Marion Rutland and daughter Tracy behind the counter with the 'For Sale Here – The Melton Book; super photos, you'll never believe it!' sign above their heads. Mr and Mrs Rutland's four children, Kit, Carol, Tracy and son James are all butchers and work in the shop.

SHERRINGTON

SHARRINGTON ALL SAINTS' CHURCH – 1920s

Sharrington is a village three miles north of Melton Constable. The church is a building of flint with stone dressings in the Early English Style. The western tower contains one bell dated 1715 and the lower part of the tower forms a porch. The Register dates from 1672 and there are brasses to John Botolff, 1476, and John Sharington, 1498. The church was restored in 1968 at the cost of Sir Alfred Jodrell of Bayfield Hall. The Rev H J Lowe was rector here from 1920–45.

THE RECTORY, SHARRINGTON – 1956

This picture shows Mrs Norah Lowe, the Rev Lowe's wife, on the lawn at the Rectory, playing croquet with her two grandsons, Johnny and Christopher. The Rectory was situated ¼ mile from the church, past the Chequers Inn, which was kept by Mr Chamberlain at the time.

ARTIE HOWARD'S GARAGE, THORNAGE

Mr Artie Howard was the owner of this garage. It is said that, as it was situated in a rather out-of-the-way place, during World War Two a member of the Home Guard was detailed to watch the petrol pumps at night, so the petrol, which was rationed, did not get stolen. Mr Howard was also the owner of a Dairy and milk rounds.

ARTIE HOWARD'S MOBILE MILK BAR – *c.* **1939**

Artie Howard's Refreshment Bar was a familiar sight at various venues including Snetterton Motor Race Track, Fakenham and Great Yarmouth Horse Race Tracks, and the Royal Norfolk Show, serving milk drinks, coffee, tea and promoting milk in general. It was built by Billy Howlett, ably assisted by John Funnell, Artie and John Howard.

QUOITS MATCH AT BRININGHAM WHITE HORSE – *c.* 1930

This occasion was a match between Briningham 'White Horse' and Briston 'Half Moon'. Sad to say, there is no indication of who won! Players are, left to right, standing: Mr Manthorpe, Joe Fuller, W Jarman, George Maidstone, Mrs Eggleton (Landlady), Mr Bird, Mr Jeary and B Coble (Briston). Seated: S Lubbock (Briston), W Eggleton (landlord), Fred Holmes, Stan Williamson, Knights Eggleton (Landlord of the Briston Half Moon).

THE SIGNALBOX, BRININGHAM

Situated about a mile from Melton Station on the Cromer line is the Briningham Single-line Junction signalbox. The laying of a double line between here and Melton Constable was completed in June 1900 facilitating the movement of trains and avoiding congestion at Melton. Mr Scarfe, who lived at the gatehouse, is seen at the door.

FARMWORKERS' OUTING, THORNAGE – Early 1990s

This very rare and collectable postcard shows the annual outing organised by Farmer George Raby of White House Farm. His workers and their families are seen here outside the barn, ready to depart for the coast. This mode of transport was the only one available at the time for Sunday School and other such outings.

THURSFORD STATION – *c.* **1925**

This station came into use when the line between Fakenham and Guestwick was opened on 19 January 1882. On weekdays, five trains per day each way ran through here, between King's Lynn and Melton. The Sunday service was one train per day each way. After leaving Thursford, the line rose to 312ft above sea-level at Piggs Grave (the highest point in the whole M&GN system), a short distance from Melton Constable Station. The Stationmaster at Thursford in 1925 was Herbert Youngman.

Picture courtesy: Philip Standley Collection.

THE BALE OAK, BALE – *c.* **1937**

Bale Oak Inn, shown here, was named after the famous Great Oak tree of immense size that stood on the Green near Bale church. It was 36ft in circumference, with one branch 75ft long. Many tales are told about it; a farmer used the hollow trunk to keep pigs in, a shoe-mender set up shop in it, and twenty-six men could stand inside it. It became so dangerous that the Lord of the Manor had it taken down in 1860 and taken to Fakenham in farm wagons.

MRS CLETHEROE, OUTSIDE WOOD DALLING 'PLOUGH' – 1929

Mr Charlie Cletheroe was landlord of the Plough Inn at this time. The picture shows his wife Martha in their ponycart outside the building. They later moved to Plumb's Cottages, Briston, now demolished. Charlie was a familiar sight in the ponycart going round the village.

GLENVIEW STORES, WOOD DALLING – 1917

Mr Eric Churchman kept these village stores at this period. It is probably Mr Churchman and his wife who are pictured in the garden outside the shop, although there was a Mr Harold Chapman also involved in the business. Mr Eric Churchman went to live in Canada after he retired, but came back to visit Wood Dalling before he died. The stores were cottages for at least sixty-five years, before recent renovation converted them into one house.

THE POST OFFICE, WOOD DALLING – 1917

Mr Eric Churchman ran the Post Office as well as Glenview Stores, with Mrs Elizabeth Churchman being the Postmistress. After he retired it was run by Mr and Mrs Gaskins for thirty years and then by their son and his wife Sheila for another forty years, closing on 7 June 2001. They had the cottages, that were originally Glenview Stores, completely renovated and moved there on that date. Mrs Sheila Gaskins' mother was Madge Attoe, *née* Roe, whose father kept Briston Waterloo House Stores in the 1920s.

Corpusty Mill Bridge swept away during flood Aug 1912

CORPUSTY MILL BRIDGE – 1912

Following the devastating 1912 floods, this postcard shows Mill Bridge having been swept right away in the disaster. The owner of the Mill at the time is thought to be Frank Carlyle Fisher who was also a baker.

CORPUSTY MILL'S NEW BRIDGE – 1914

This smart new bridge was built to replace the one destroyed in the 1912 floods. Some time later the Mill was taken over by C J C Lee.

THE TOLL BRIDGE, GUIST – *c.* 1910

In this rare postcard, the single arch bridge over the River Wensum can be seen behind the Tollgate. Tolls were taken by Mrs Nelson (believed to be the lady taking the Toll charge from the cyclist) and her son Josiah. The Tollgate belonged to Mr William Norris JP of Wood Norton.

THE STREET, HINDOLVESTON – *c.* 1912

A charming rural village scene of The Street looking east, with local children posing for the photograph. The gentleman with the horse is believed to be Arthur Pratt, farmer, standing outside his premises. The row of cottages behind him are now demolished.

MR HOLSEY, HINDOLVESTON – 1922

This photograph of Mr Holsey at the back of his ironmongery cart was taken by the Rev John Atkins Easten MA, Rector at Thurning church and father of the Rev Edmund John Attlee Easten MA, Rector from 1961. The cart is seen here outside the Rectory during the summer of 1922.

Picture courtesy: Peter Jackson.

HINDOLVESTON SILVER BAND – *c.* 1940s

The wartime new 'Utility' bus belongs to Mr Arthur Holsey of Hindolveston. The driver, who also played in the band, was Mr Sonny Fisher (second left). David Scott, in his army uniform, is seen third from the right. Note there were three girls in the Band. 'Utility' was the name given to goods manufactured during World War Two and was stamped on furniture.

SCHOOL CORNER, HINDOLVESTON – *p.u.* **1915**

H J Green of Norwich was the Architect of the Public Elementary School for 160 children, built in 1889. At the time of this picture, the Headmaster was Frederick Hockham who occupied the School House; Charles Beane, the Assistant Master, lived at 'The Retreat' and Miss Maud Crisp was the Infants' Mistress. Closed, like so many other village schools, it stands on the corner of Melton Road. Message on the back of card reads: "Can you pick out Doris on this picture?"

THE RETREAT, HINDOLVESTON – *p.u.* **1911**

Mr Beane, the assistant Schoolmaster, lived here at this time. It is almost certainly his wife standing at the gate. Around 1880, Shadrach William Skillings kept the General Shop here. He was also a Hawker. Mrs Susannah Codling kept the shop seen on the right in the adjoining premises, at the time this picture was taken. The Retreat stands almost opposite the School.

ALEXANDER ABERDEIN'S SHOP, HINDOLVESTON – *c.* 1903

Mr Aberdein commenced trading in the late 1800s as a grocer, draper, boot-warehouseman and Insurance Agent, it is thought with financial assistance from others, hence the name-board 'Aberdein & Company'. The young man, holding the horse's head, is his assistant Mr A C Barsted, born in 1888. This shop is now tastefully converted into a modern bungalow, retaining the main stepped-feature, and is called 'Crowsteps'. Alexander Aberdein had a second shop, in the old National School, run by Miss Ivy Aberdein. This was taken over in 1947 by Mr and Mrs Leslie Wakefield. Alexander Aberdein's father Samuel had also been a grocer and draper in the village since the early 1870s.

GARDEN STAFF AT MELTON CONSTABLE HALL – *c.* **1897–1900**

Pictured here are Arthur Strike, said to be an expert at growing grapes, front row seated, second left in bowler hat. He came from Hindolveston. Far right standing, is Laurence Eke. Beside him holding the pot plant is Herbert Fisher, aged about 15 at the time, and standing behind him is Alfred Brett. These three also lived in Hindolveston. Alfred Brett and Herbert Fisher had witnessed the collapse of Hindolveston church tower a few years earlier.

ST PETER'S CHURCH, MELTON CONSTABLE – *c.* 1913

Standing in Melton Constable Park, this small parish church, seating 100, is a distance from the village. It is a very ancient building, consecrated in 1092 and built of Hunstanton stone, in mixed styles, with a central Norman tower with one bell. The Church was completely restored at the sole expense of Sir George Astley, the 20th Lord Hastings, in 1885. In 1921, a Marble Tablet was erected in memory of the parishioners who died in World War One. The Rector at the time of this picture was Rev Arthur Hedley Crowe MD and the church Register dates from 1551.

MELTON CONSTABLE PARK AND SWANTON NOVERS W.I. – *c.* **1937**

Some of the ladies of the village Women's Institute are picture here in their costumes for the sketch they performed at the Maddermarket Theatre, Norwich, on 1 December, 1937. Entitled *All on a Summers Day in 1830*, the cast, reading left to right are: standing, Mrs Sheckalls, The Hon. Jean Astley, Nellie S Withers and Mrs Cossey. Seated, Mrs Ross Webb and Mrs Gidney.

The Station, Melton Constable.

STATION PLATFORM, MELTON – *c.* 1924

Looking down from the station approach, over the goods yard there is a clear view of the platform with the 3rd class Waiting Room on the right and Refreshment Rooms next to it. Posters advertising Mablethorpe, Lowestoft and 'Midland – the best route to Belfast' and Furness Railway to the English Lakes are seen, with Royal Assurance and Shipping Line posters above. The roof of one of the engine sheds is visible over the canopy.

MR RIBBANS, TICKET COLLECTOR, MELTON STATION

This picture shows Mr Ribbans, ticket-punch in his hand, on the platform outside the ticket office, which was reached from the road by a stone stairway. Tickets were green in colour about 1in x 2¼in in size – whole tickets for single journeys and returns were split in half. There was a system of privilege tickets for widows and families of former employees, the fares being extremely reasonable, ie a season ticket covering school term from Melton Constable to Fakenham Hempton Station was about 11/- (52¼p) and this included Saturday morning journeys for tennis or hockey matches at Fakenham Secondary School.

MELTON CONSTABLE RAILWAY POLICE

This is a picture of Mr Peck, one of the three or four Railway Police. Others were Mr Saddler, Tom Bond and Jesse Brown. Their duties consisted of 3 x 8-hour shifts, looking round the works at night, punching their clock cards into the Time Clock every hour to prove they'd been round.

MR MARRIOTT'S TRAVELLING OFFICE – *c.* **1920**

Mr Marriott used this Railway Carriage as his office when overseeing projects at various places along the M&GN network. Some of the gentlemen pictured are: Jesse Brown, Mr Langley, Mr Marriott, B Newman and the guard, Mr A Fuller.

OFFICE BLOCK, MELTON WORKS – Late 1960s

The offices on the far left belonged to Mr Marriott and his Head Clerk, Edgar Palmer. Amongst the other clerks was Mr Teddy Eke, who was teased with 'silly' telephone calls by the other clerks, due to his high squeaky voice. As the tale is told, one morning the calls had been particularly bad and next time the 'phone rang he let fly with some choice expletives including some four-letter words, but it was Mr Marriott on the other end of the line, and he promptly gave poor Teddy the sack for using bad language!

TRAVELLING CRANE, MELTON – *c.* **1937**

A part of the M&GN's service stock, this six-wheeled travelling-crane was thought to have been originally built for the Eastern & Midlands Railway in about 1884. Its number was 491, and it was used for all kinds of heavy lifting work. Coal trucks and wagons can be seen in the goods yard to the rear.

Picture courtesy: Mr R Casserley.

THE ENGINE TURNTABLE, MELTON – Date unknown

The engine would be driven onto the turntable and the driver and fireman would manually turn it to face in the other direction, each pushing a lever on opposite sides. The turntable was so well-lubricated that on occasions it was seen to be operated by one man only – much to the amazement of local children waiting for their school trains. A new turntable was installed only a short time before the Railway closed.

ENGINE CLEANERS, MELTON WORKS – *c.* 1939

One of the dirtiest jobs on the railways, was cleaning the engines, but the men all took great pride in their work. The gentlemen pictured here, on a newly-refurbished engine (note the shiny wheels), are Mr 'Snigger' Miller (second left), the others are thought to be, left to right: Mr Taberham, Mr Rutland (with moustache), Mr Reeve and Mr Miller, who lived at Briston and was also a member of the Briston Silver Band.

CROMER CRAB TRAIN – 1 July 1936

This train has just arrived from Cromer. The guard on the left, going off duty, is Mr Jack Childs holding his wicker lunch basket in his left hand. Mr George Cork is pushing the barrow loaded with Cromer crabs, next is Mr Frary, always very smart and always wearing a button hole. The man standing near the engine is Mr Leslie Cousins and the man bending over on the tender is Mr Fred Eke. The engine appears to be a Johnson Class C440.

Picture courtesy: Mr R Casserley.

M&GNJRPS SPECIAL – *c.* **1960**

The M&GN Joint Railway Preservation Society ran several 'Special' trains after the closure of the line to passenger traffic. This unusual view was photographed from the vicinity of Melton West signalbox and shows the train standing in Melton Station on 21 May 1960. The engine used was J1, 0-6-0, 65469. Although passenger service had ceased some time earlier the Melton–Sheringham Service survived until 4 April 1964 pulled by diesels.

MR STRANGLEMAN AND HIS GANGERS – Date unknown

Mr Strangleman, who lived at Briston, is seen here on the right with his gang of twenty-five men who repaired the rails and also laid new tracks. Based at Melton Constable, the gang was one of several others on the M&GN network.

ENGINE No. 047 at WEYBOURNE STATION – Date unknown

The driver of 047, on this occasion, was Mr Drury and Sam Adams was fireman. The loco is believed to have been at Weybourne when the photograph was taken. Many people felt great sadness at the passing of the wonderful old steam trains. Later diesel engines took over but they didn't have the same character or individuality.

THE TRAIN NOW STANDING, CROMER BEACH STATION – 1955

The driver and fireman, George Dack and 'Nibs' Earl, in the engine cab, about to depart for Melton Constable. Engine No. 43095 was a comparatively modern engine, being built in 1951.

CLOSE UP OF ENGINE No. 43095 AT CROMER BEACH STATION – 1955

This picture was taken same day, same journey, as the previous page, but showing George Dack and Bert (Nibs) Earl in greater detail.

OLD MACHINE SHOP, MELTON WORKS – *c.* **1976**

This picture shows the old machine shop at Melton, then being used by the Bedford firm Brookhurst Igranic, also as a machine shop, making switch gear. The man in the far background is George Woodcock from Melton. The man in the white coat is Alan Lambert from Fakenham and on the lathe is Rick Mann also of Fakenham.

Picture courtesy: Peter Jackson.

GEORGE DACK ON THE SLITTER MACHINE, MELTON – Late 1980s

Cutler Hammer had taken over from Brookhurst Igranic when this photo of George Dack on the Slitter Machine was taken. It was used for making electrical components for resistors (*seen on following page*). Eaton Ltd took over the firm after Cutler Hammer.

LOADING RESISTORS AT CUTLER HAMMER, MELTON – Late 1980s

The finished product of resistors being loaded for dispatch at Cutler Hammer's premises at the old Melton works site. Pictured are, left to right; Denny Twiddy, Ron Derek, Melly Allison on the fork lift truck, and George Woodcock standing behind.

MR A W COOTER'S SHOP – 15 September 1913

Situated at the corner of Burgh Beck Road and Briston Road was Arthur Wilfred Cooter's Drapers, Milliners and Outfitters shop. As can be seen by all the window bills, an 'After Season' sale was in progress. The premises later became the Co-operative Society's Drapery Department. Mr George William Fisher's Chemist's Shop was at the right-hand end of the building. He was also a maker of artificial teeth and sold photographic equipment. The premises today are a Minimarket and Fish & Chip shop.

MAIN STREET, MELTON CONSTABLE – 1930s

The Co-op Grocery and General Store is seen on the left of the picture. The upper storey being used for meetings. The Co-op Drapery was at the bottom of the hill on the left. Rose's Bakery handcart is on the way back to the Bakery after making deliveries.

MAIN STREET, MELTON CONSTABLE – 1930s

This picture was taken near the point where Melton meets Briston. In the centre distance the row of Council Houses is just in view, whilst on the right is Mr W (Chemical Bill) Fisher's Chemists Shop. The railed-in piece of land on the right is where the Doctor's Surgery now stands. This picture was taken the same day as the previous one, as Rose's Bakery handcart can be seen making progress towards its point in the previous picture.

MR CLITHEROE, HAIRDRESSER, MELTON

Mr Clitheroe's shop was in the wooden building at the bottom of Melton Hill, opposite the Co-op Drapery Store. It had formerly belonged to Pask the Tailors who made livery for the staff at Melton Constable Hall. By the signs on the walls it appears Mr Clitheroe also sold tobacco and cigarettes. The water for shaves and shampoos was heated on a meths stove. He kept his prices in line with Mr George Eke, the hairdresser at the top of the hill – price of a shave, shampoo and haircut being sixpence at this time. This was so they didn't poach each others customers. The shop closed in 1964.

MR RICHES' BUTCHERS SHOP, MELTON CONSTABLE

Mr E T Riches had an impressive display of meat and sausages in his window. It is believed to be Mr Riches and his wife in the doorway of the shop in Gordon Road. It was then taken over by Mr Warnes, for whom Bertie Graves (*page 60*) worked for a time and after that Mr Williamson became the Butcher. Finally, this is the shop where Mr Michael Rutland started out in business, before taking over the Post Office building in the Main Street, where he is today.

G VARDIGAN'S CHIP SHOP, MELTON CONSTABLE – *c.* 1951

Mr Geoffrey Vardigan's Fish and Chip shop was at the end of Burgh Beck Road. His brother Stanley can be seen leaning against the front of his car, in front of the shop.

MELTON SUNDAY SCHOOL OUTING – 1939

This was the last Melton Railway Mission Sunday School Outing, by rail to Cromer, before the Second World War began. Civilians were banned from beaches after they were fortified against invasion by Germany. Mr G B Clarke, Secretary to the Sunday School, is in the dark suit (second row from the top), and Jack Gaskin, the Superintendent, is just below him. During the war, the children were taken to Melton Constable Park for their outing instead of Cromer.

GORDON ROAD, MELTON CONSTABLE – 1914

This postcard was sent by a Sgt Drake who was billeted in the house on the left he has marked with an 'x', on 1 December 1914. Mr Cooter's Drapery Store is just off the picture to the right. This was later to become the Co-op Drapery Store run by Miss Debbie Stimpson, who later had her own Wool Shop in Bull Street, Holt. Her parents also lived in one of the houses on the left.

HERBERT GEORGE STOLWORTHY

Mr Stolworthy was a long-standing resident of Melton, moving there from Great Yarmouth in the 1880s. He was Works Manager of the Signal and Works Department of the M&GN Railway depot at Melton Constable and overseer to the parish and a member of the Parish Council. He came from a prominent Great Yarmouth family of millwrights responsible, among other things, for building the Berney Arms Mill. Mr Stolworthy died in 1919 during the Spanish 'Flu epidemic and was buried in St Peter's churchyard.

WEDDING RECEPTION AT No. 1 GROVE HOUSE – 1908

Taken in the garden of No. 1 Grove House, this photograph shows the reception of the wedding between Stanley Webber and Constance Amelia Stolworthy in 1908. The bride's father, Mr Herbert Stolworthy, stands far left. The groom's father, Mr George Webber, stands on the back row next to the bride's brothers, wearing bowler hats. Mr Stolworthy was an employee of the M&GN Railway and Mr Webber owned the General Stores at Briston. This photo was donated by the grandson of one of the bride's sisters, Miss Dora Stolworthy, 18 years old, sitting on left of the picture with flowers in her lap. The house later became occupied by Dr John Meanly. *Picture courtesy: Mr C M Blake.*

BRISTON ROAD, MELTON CONSTABLE – June 1916

This postcard shows the Railway Mission Hall centre, and Mr May, Headmaster of Melton and Briston Higher Standard School, lived in one of the houses to the left. On the right-hand side of the picture the panelling probably indicates that the house called 'The Nest' was being built at this time, or the District Nurse's house.

MR BERTIE GRAVES, BAKER'S BOY, BRISTON – 1926

Bertie Graves was born in Southborough and came to Briston aged 16½ years and with 3/6d in his pocket to work for Mr Bushell the baker, of Melton Road, Briston. He lodged with Mrs M Broughton at the time. He next worked for Roses the Bakers on Melton High Street and after that worked for Warnes the Butchers in Gordon Road. He was then in the RAF for 6½ years before taking over Mr Harry Pilch's Butchers Shop, Briston, on his own account in the late 1940s.

OLD COTTAGES, CROSSWAYS FARM CORNER

These old cottages were demolished to make way for new housing. To the far left were Nurseries kept by Mr Yull. The road at base of the photograph is from Briston village centre, turn left for Melton Constable and right for the road to Norwich. Carter's farm pit was on the right and Stacey's Farm on the left at the bottom of the picture.

Picture courtesy: Peter Jackson.

THRESHING AT CROSSWAYS FARM, BRISTON – *c.* **1929**

A rare postcard of Knights Eggleton's steam engine and threshing tackle at work on Mr J S Carter's farm. Mr Carter is seen on the left of picture and his young son John beside Knights Eggleton on the right. Farmers usually had a tank of water and a load of steam-coal ready for the arrival of the engine and supplied the Contractor with enough coal to get to his next destination. Today the Combine Harvester does the harvesting instead. Sacks were often printed with the farmer's name and the date. A sack dated 1912 can be seen centre-picture – they were quite expensive, about 1/- each in those times, but very durable.

POPPY DAY COLLECTORS, BRISTON – Mid 1930s

Miss Olive Juby organised the Poppy Day Collection for British Legion funds every year. The ladies are, first left: Mrs Middleton (Mr Higginbottoms' Housekeeper), next could be Mrs Ivy Sexton, then Miss Olive Juby, next Mrs Adams, next Mrs Wilton Jun. and finally Mrs Wilton Sen.

FANCY DRESS PARADE, BRISTON – 1935

This picture was taken in the garden of Mrs Juby's residence 'The Poplars' before joining the Parade. First left is Miss Irene Hewitt, next is Mrs Ginny Juby, then Evelyn Graveling. The young man next is believed to be Mr Butters; then Mrs Garrood, next Gerald Woode, beside him with eye patch is thought to be Morgan Kendle, next Miss Olive Juby and finally Martha Cletheroe.

Picture courtesy: Mrs Rene Mendham.

MR BERTIE GRAVES, BUTCHER, BRISTON – 1958

Mr Graves is seen outside his shop at Briston, after a particularly heavy fall of snow. He continued here in the butchery business until he died aged 87 years in February 1988. His grandsons took over, continuing till the present day.

VETERANS OF BRISTON SALVATION ARMY

Strongly represented in Briston, the Salvation Army first held meetings in the little hall down the lane leading to the church back gate. Sufficient funds were gathered to build their own hall which stands on the opposite side of the road where the Post Office is today. Pictured here are left to right, back row: Bert Reynolds, Herbert Drewry, Mr Fulcher and Albert Rudd. Front row: Walter Wright, Mrs Wright, Jim Porter and William Ellis.

LECTURE HALL CORNER, BRISTON – *c.* 1910

The Congregational Minister, Rev Herbert Shellabear, occupied the Manse, facing the centre of the picture at this time. The shop to the left was Henry Pilch the Butchers. Mr Pilch was said to be related to the famous Norfolk cricketer, Fuller Pilch. The shop on the left, with the bridle hanging on the wall, was Henry Rudd & Son, Saddlers and Harness Makers. The road past the Manse leads to the Lanes and the Lecture Hall is to the right of the Manse.

GREENGROCERY DELIVERIES, BRISTON – *c.* **1954**

Born in Briningham, Ted Wright helped his father, Sid, with the fruit and vegetable deliveries from an early age. The family moved the business to Briston in 1949 to the shop that had been Mrs Cobles sweet shop and Ted (aged 16 years) is seen here with the faithful pony 'Betty' pulling the cart, at Woodfields, Briston.

'NORFOLK HOUSE', BRISTON – 1929

Norfolk House is situated opposite the Oddfellows' Hall. Mr George Hewitt lived there after retiring as landlord of the Chequers Inn. He continued his coal business from the back of the premises. He and his second wife Rhona (standing right) are seen here with their car, one of only a few private vehicles in Briston at the time. A 'BP' petrol can and a spare wheel are strapped to the running board.

SPORTS DAY, BRISTON – *c.* **1931**

The Annual Sports were held in conjunction with Briston May Fair, on the meadow behind Norfolk House. This year was a special occasion, as a Troop of Indian Senior Scouts attended, with their leader, Hardiel Singh, during their tour of England. They can be seen at the front of the picture, with Mrs Ida Carter on the right. Seated beside her is Miss Nora Cooke, Mr J S Carter is on the far left and Mr F J Higginhottom centre back row. Many other names are known, but space does not allow inclusion.

BRISTON FLOWER SHOW – 1929

This flower show took place on Mr George Hewitt's meadow, at the back of Norfolk House. The picture shows the refreshment stall, situated in a cartshed, in case of rain. Hygiene regulations were not what they are today, but the ladies look very happy in their wonderful assortment of hats. Left to right, they are: Mrs Adams, Mrs Pestell, Mrs S Reynolds, Muriel Eggleton, Mrs Rice, Mrs Knights Eggleton, Katie Willmott, Mrs Mabel Rice, Mrs Strutt and Marjory Rice.

WHIST DRIVE AND DANCE, BRISTON – *c.* **1930**

This event was held at the end of the whist-drive season. Organised by Miss Olive Juby each year, it took place in the Oddfellows' Hall. Miss Juby is seen third from the left on the front row, with Mrs Spencer from Hunworth, the Guest of Honour, on her right. Her bouquet had been presented by the little girl in the white dress. Among others on the photo are: Madge Rowe, Evelyn Graveling, Sid Reynolds and his wife, Trixie and Beryl Phillips, Roger Brown and his wife Norah, Stanley Fisher, Jean Juby, Mrs Ginny Juby and numerous others, which is hoped some readers will recognise.

THE 'VAGABONDS' DANCE BAND, BRISTON – *c.* **1939**

This popular band played at dances in Briston and surrounding villages. Here, they are on stage at Briston Oddfellows' Hall. Members are Sydney Youngs, violin (seated), Eddy Wilkinson, violin, Basil Dix on drums and Eric Church at the piano. Briston had a second dance band at this time run by Sidney Reynolds Jun. and called 'The Serenaders'.

BRISTON POST OFFICE – *c. 1950s*

This side view of Stanley and Albert Howes' Post Office shows a Parkinsons Pills advert covering the whole of the side of the building. It is doubtful if such advertising would be permitted today. Garrood's Bakery is seen on the left, while the little lane running to the church back gate goes down past the front of the Post Office and the road going past the cottages leads to the village centre. The Post Office is now demolished,the corner re-routed and the lane leads to a large new estate that goes round the back of the churchyard and comes out in Hall Street beside the 'Grange'.

Picture courtesy: Eastern Daily Press.

REMAINS OF BRISTON 'HONEY CART' – 1970s

Younger readers will always have enjoyed the luxury of indoor flush toilets, but older ones will remember the outside toilets (sometimes a long way down the garden) with a wooden seat and a pail below, which was emptied once a week by the man on the night cart. The remains of Briston night cart were found by Peter Jackson of Briston, under the tanks at Melton Works while he was photographing the station buildings before demolition in the 1970s, the metal tank having rotted away (no wonder!). The driver was Bobby Tann, who lived near Briston Post Office,

MR GEORGE HEWITT, COAL MERCHANT, BRISTON – 1920s

As well as being landlord of the Chequers Inn, Mr Hewitt ran a thriving coal-merchants business. Three of his loaded coal-carts are seen here standing in the Chequers yard, ready to deliver coal around Briston and surrounding area. Mr Hewitt is seated in the pony trap second right. Two of the drivers are Charlie Bligh, from West End, and Mr Smithson, who lived in the terrace at the rear of the picture.

CHEQUERS INN, BRISTON – *c.* **1900**

Landlord George Hewitt stands on the right. His wife to the left, beside her their son Sidney, who was to take over the tenancy in 1910. On the left is 'Tash' Twiddy who lived in a cottage opposite the Blacksmith's shop. He looked after the horses belonging to Mr Plumb at Clarence House.

CHURCH STREET, BRISTON – *p.u.* 1934

This postcard is included as it is the only one obtainable with (part of) the front of Stanley and Albert Howes' Post Office. The milk cart belonged to Mr J S Carter, Crossways' Farm, with white pony 'Peggy' between the shafts. Barclays Bank in the Terrace on the right, opened once a week for two hours on a Friday, in the front room of the home of Mr and Mrs Wilson.

WATERLOO HOUSE GROCERY AND DRAPERY STORE, BRISTON – 1920s

Mr Arthur Roe kept these stores in the 1920s, taking over from Mr Webber. Everything in the grocery line could be bought there, from paraffin to goods like dried fruit and sago, all weighed out in thick blue conical shaped bags. Farmer's Glory and Force were the breakfast cereals at this time. On the drapery side all goods from underwear, dresses, socks and stockings to hats were obtainable. Mr Roe had a daughter Madge, and son Gerald, who sadly died aged eleven years. Sid Reynolds had a bicycle shop at the right-hand end of the building.

ERNIE RICHES, BRISTON BARBER – *c. 1930*

Wounded in World War One, Mr Riches started his Barber's Shop after the war. It was situated on the opposite side of the road to the church gates. Unisex Hair Salons are not such a new thing, as Mr Riches trimmed boys, girls, ladies and gents hair – giving gents a shave as well! He charged 2d to trim a boys hair and would often give the lad a penny back. He sealed the ends of girls and ladies hair with a lighted taper.

MISS JULIA HILL, CHURCH STREET, BRISTON – *c.* 1917

Miss Hill lived in the end house opposite Billy Godfrey's fish shop. She had come to live in Briston about 1914. Her father was a coal importer who lived in the Red House on Blakeney Quay. As the years went on she began to lose her memory and forgot things. She would sit on her front doorstep on a chair, with a 'frail' (rush basket) beside her and ask one of the local children to go up to Bertie Barwick's, the taxi driver, to come and take her to Melton Station as she was going to Australia to visit her brother. Mr Barwick would say: "Tell her that will be alright" – having been given the same message several time before. Miss Hill had a manx cat which she left to the author.

MR TEDDY EKE – Date unknown

Mr Eke, always a smart little man, with a bow-tie, could be seen with his wife around the village pushing their daughter Ethel, lying in a full length wickerwork invalid carriage. It is said that when her parents died Ethel got up and walked as normal. Mr Eke, as seen in the picture, was a keen violin player. He lived in the opposite end of the buildings where Miss Hill lived.

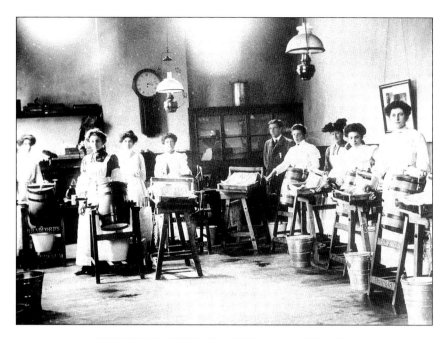

BUTTER-MAKING CLASSES, BRISTON – 1910

This butter-making class took place in the Reading Room, which was situated in the yard beside Mrs Cobles sweet shop at Briston. Note the seven individual butter churns. Nearly all were operated by ladies from different branches of the Williamson families, all of which had farms in Briston. The lady second from the left is Mrs Alfred Williamson of Frogmore Farm. In the 1920s–30s a Mr Stoner attended at the Reading Room once a month, mending watches and clocks. He always arrived by motorbike and sidecar – the sidecar resembling a silver torpedo!

BRISTON CYCLE CLUB PARADE – *c.* 1908

At the turn of the century, cycling had become a very popular pastime and many villages formed their own Cycling Clubs, organising events such as Fancy Dress Parades and Races. Seen here, outside his house, before the 1908 Fancy Dress Parade, is Briston Public Elementary School Headmaster, Mr Thomas Robinson, dressed as Ally Sloper with two of his children – an Arab Sheik and Little Miss Muffet. Mr Robinson used this card as a Christmas card for Christmas 1908. He continued as Headmaster of the School, and his wife as Infants' Mistress, until 1929, when Mr Thomas Bray took over the post.

VILLAGE CENTRE, BRISTON – *p.u.* **1908**

Part of Mr Robinson's – the Primary School Headmaster – house is seen far left. The Half Moon Inn, displaying a large wooden signboard 'Morgans Wines & Spirits', is next. George Fish was landlord at this time. Next is the Blacksmiths, and next to that Mrs Cobles' sweet shop, which housed the village Reading Room in its yard. Far right is Clarence House, built by James Plumb in 1896 on the site of three cottages. Now occupied by Mr and Mrs Daniels it remains almost unaltered from Victorian times. It is said that one of the men employed to build the house – a Mr Batterbee from Wood Dalling – walked to Briston daily, using the railway line as a more direct route, but one day was unfortunately killed by a train.

CHURCH STREET, BRISTON – Late 1920s/early 1930s

On the right is the garden to 'Tash' Twiddy's cottage. The right-hand end of the large building was occupied by Teddy Eke, whilst Miss Julia Hill lived in the other end. Reynolds petrol pumps are seen just above the man walking. Part of Aubrey Terrace is in the centre, then the trees behind the churchyard wall. The small white cottage adjoining was occupied by Mr and Mrs Ives and their son Clifford, but it was soon to be demolished. The house next was where Mr Billy Godfrey eventually opened his Fish and Chip shop and next is where Mr Burgess, former Bandmaster, and his wife lived. Then comes Mrs Cobles' sweetshop and finally the Blacksmith's yard. The picture was taken from edge of the Village Green.

BRISTON SCHOOL FOOTBALL TEAM – *c.* 1930

This picture shows Mr Thomas Bray, the School Headmaster, on the right. The team are, back row, from left to right: Albert Whittred, Dick Daniels, Harry Perry, Jimmy Miller, (?) Rayner. Middle row: Kenny Whittred, Derek Barham, (?) Taberham, Bertie Kidd, (?) Grint. Front row: Kenny Rolffe, Mickey Graveling, W Perry.

Mr Bray had a Clino car with a 'dickey' at the rear. It was the Author's first ride in a car in this vehicle, on a picnic to Thurning Wood, aged five years old.

Picture courtesy: Peter Jackson.

CLASS AT BRISTON SCHOOL – 1929/30

Names listed, back row, left to right: Reggie Barham, Fred Perry, Douglas Basted, Ted Whittred, Bob Kidd, Owen Whittred. Middle row, left to right: David Willimott, Phyllis Scott, Dorothy Cushion, Arthur Willimott, Kenneth Scott, Harry Lubbock, Alan Adams, William Norton and Herbert Thornton. Front row, left to right: Grace Williamson, Isobel Reynolds, Phyllis Scarfe, Irene Hewitt, Sylvia Smith, Joan Riches, Molly Barwick.

Picture courtesy: Molly Barwick.

CLASS AT BRISTON SCHOOL – *c.* 1947

Back row standing, left to right: Margaret Abbs, Michael Hagon, Antony Baldock, Lionel Adams, Buddy Barham, Ray Rolph, Herbert Jackson, John Myhill, Robin Daniels, Philip Dagless and Alfred Wiggins. Middle row, left to right: Lorna Stearman, Margaret Buck, Ann Wegg, John Hardingham, Norman Eggleton, Reginald Bunkel, Ray Lubbock, Peter Bayfield, Windsor Whittred, Peter Unglass, Maurice Hall and Douglas Kidd. Front row seated, left to right: Connie Lubbock, Marion Graves, Jenny Barber, Doreen Smith, Eileen Kidd, Joy Colmon, Nancy Gibbons, Doreen Grand, Lilly Perry, Shirley Doy, Petty Ward, Pauline Bunkel and Pat Beckett. *Picture courtesy: Peter Jackson.*

MRS CULLEY, CHURCH STORES, BRISTON

Mrs Kate Culley kept the Church Stores in Church Street. Her house was set back from the road next to the churchyard. The shop was a maroon-painted, corrugated-iron structure, but had a beautiful mahogany shop fitting inside, with different sized drawers with things like 'sultanas' and 'rice' etc painted on in gold paint. There was a Macfarlane Langs' cake case on the counter, with large slabs of fruit, plain and angel cake inside. These could be cut into whatever size the customer required. After she retired Mr and Mrs Gaskin took over the shop, which is now demolished.

BRISTON W.I. OUTING – Summer 1939

This photograph of the Briston Women's Institute outing was taken at its destination – Skegness. Back row, left to right, ladies standing: Miss Maggie Graveling, Mrs Taylor, Mrs Fox, Mrs Mary Howard, Mrs Garrood, Mrs S Hewitt. The next four names suggested are Mrs Wilkinson, Mrs Adams, Mrs B Barwick and Mrs R Jex. Fourth from the right is Mrs Godfrey, then Miss Shingler, Mrs Reynolds, Alan Adams and Mrs R Eke. Front row, seated, left to right: Martha Cletheroe, Mrs LeGrys, Mrs G Mack, Mrs Futter, Mrs Knights Eggleton, Mrs Coble and Mrs R Rudd.

HALL ROAD, BRISTON.

DEVONSHIRE HOUSE, HALL STREET, BRISTON

This postcard was sent to Mrs A Palmer, 7 Ferndale Terrace, Melton Constable, from Mr Bambridge, the occupant of Devonshire House, asking her not to come for her eggs in the afternoon but leave it until the evening. Date appears to be 1922 on the postmark! The main road goes down to the Village Centre, the school green being on the right past the hedge. The lane leading to the left went through to Ridland's Farm and just inside on the left was a small square beck, with lovely clear water, always full of 'tiddlers'.

TAKING THE RAILWAY TRACK UP, BRISTON – 1960

A desolate scene showing the track-removal train at Ridland's Bridge. In years gone by, crowded excursion trains were seen passing through on the way to Great Yarmouth. The meadow (right) was a favourite place where local children fished for 'tiddlers' in the stream. I recall doing this with Beryl and Mary, Johnnie and Eddy Watts. The weather always seemed sunny. The engine drivers would blow their whistle and wave to us as they thundered by. The road under the bridge leads to Ridland's Farm and Bluebell Woods.

Picture courtesy: Dick Barwick.

CORONATION SOUVENIR, BRISTON – 12 May 1937

Most names can be remembered. Back row, from left: S Reynolds Jun., unknown, S Eggleton, Mrs Garood, Bertie Barwick, unknown, unknown. George Norton, Ida Carter, Mr Wilkins, M/S Sexton, S Reynolds Sen., unknown, unknown, Hilda Fisher, Grace Williamson, Mr Higginbottom in between them. Rest of back row unknown, except for Mr Futter, Headmaster of School, Mrs Smithson and Eric Dack. Front row: first two unknown, next Mrs Sexton, Headmaster's wife, Mrs Hall the Minister's wife, Olive Juby, Ida Pilch, unknown, Mrs Bunkell and Mr Jack Carter holding flag in front. Photograph taken outside Pavilion on the 'Rec'.

MR BERTIE BARWICK AND HIS HORSE WAGONETTE

Bertie Barwick in his wagonette with his pony 'Tommy' outside cottages in Hall Street, Briston. He was disabled in World War One and started a business transporting people to and from Melton Constable Station and elsewhere, until the business got too much for the pony, so he switched to Citroen motor taxis. The cottages were demolished and No. 149 Hall Street now stands there.

Picture courtesy: Molly & Dick Barwick.

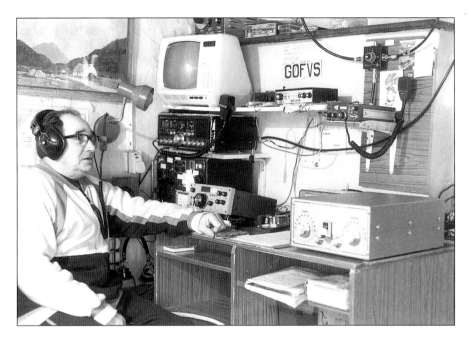

PETER JACKSON, AMATEUR RADIO OPERATOR, BRISTON – 1987

Mr Jackson is justly proud that, despite having practically no education after eleven-years-of-age, he took the examination in Radio Electronics and passed both parts with Distinction, City of Guilds of the London Institute. He also passed the Morse Code test with the Department of Board of Trade and obtained a Class A Licence. Since then he has operated world-wide, gaining many friends. He has written four booklets; the first one being *Memories of Thurning Village* which shows his love of nature and the countryside. The second is about his time in the RAF and the others are not yet printed.

Mr Jackson is a man of many talents; model making, photography and the latest being bookbinding – all self-taught.

REEPHAM ROAD CROSSING, BRISTON

Photographed around the time of the M&GN network closure this shows the Gatehouse occupied in earlier years by Mrs Colman, who always wore a man's cap, long skirts and heavy boots when opening and closing the gates. The gentleman in the picture is Mr Edwards. The line ran from Melton Constable to Great Yarmouth.

GATEKEEPER AT REEPHAM ROAD CROSSING – *c.* **1920s, early '30s**

Mrs Colman pictured here on the steps of the signalbox with her daughter and little pet dog. As can be seen Mrs Colman always wore a man's cap and also men's boots when performing her duties of opening and shutting the railway crossing gates.

Picture courtesy: Peter Jackson.

MR G E WEGG, CARPENTER, BUILDER, UNDERTAKER, BRISTON – *c.* 1942

Mr George Wegg had his premises on the Reepham Road, having come to Briston in the early 1930s. He built Briston Post Office for Stanley and Albert Howe as well as a pair of cottages in Hall Street – one occupied by Mr and Mrs Sidney Eggleton. This picture shows Mr Wegg, hammer in hand, with his eldest daughter Ann, born 1937. His younger daughter was Muriel, born 1943. His son Bob (*inset picture*) took over the business in 1947 when his father died at the young age of sixty-two. Mr Wegg was also a wheelwright.

MR G E WEGG'S PREMISES, REEPHAM ROAD, BRISTON – *c.* **1945**

Situated on the right-hand side of Reepham Road going towards Thurning were Mr Wegg's workshops. There were two saw-pits in the grounds. The nameboard reads 'G E Wegg & Son, Builders & Contractors, Plumbers, House Decorators'. Mr Wegg was also an Undertaker.

MR FOX'S SHOP, CRAYMERE, BRISTON – *c.* **1922**

Mr Fox kept the Cottage Store on the right of the picture. The lady in the doorway is Mrs Easten who had just been on a shopping trip – the Rev J A Easten being Vicar of Thurning. The cottages are facing towards Craymere Beck. This outlying part of Briston is on the borders of Thurning and Hindolveston. Note the cycle with trailer-chair in which the Rev Easten towed Mrs Easten about.

Picture courtesy: Mr Peter Jackson.

CRAYMORE BECK, BRISTON.

CRAYMERE BECK, BRISTON – *p.u.* **1909**

A peaceful rural scene at Craymere, an outlying little community, part of Briston bordering Thurning and Hindolveston. To the left, Craymere Road leads to the main part of the village, via the Reepham Road railway crossing and Hall Street. The lane to the right leads to the Mill at Watermere. The roof of the Plough Inn is seen on the skyline. The view remains much the same, but the stream now runs under the road. The little lad on the rail is Teddy Massingham.

WATERMERE, BRISTON

This idyllic rural scene shows the watermill in the background with Mr Jack Wheatley in his punt. The young lady with him is thought to be his daughter. The mill was on the border between Thurning and Briston.

THE LAWNS, EDGEFIELD ROAD, BRISTON – 1939

Mr Frederick J Higginbottom retired to 'The Lawns' after a long and distinguished working life in journalism. He wrote the book The Vivid Life, a Journalist's Career published in 1934, at Briston. He was born on 21 October 1859 at Accrington and began work for W H Smith & Sons, Castle Street, London, before moving on as reporter to the Liverpool Daily Post and several London Newspapers. He spent much time in Ireland reporting on the Troubles and ended up as Editor of the Pall Mall Gazette in 1909, associating with famous people such as Mr Asquith and Lord Astor. He took an active part in Briston village life and was a great benefactor to the community.

FLOWERS THAT BLOOM IN SPRING, EDGEFIELD – 1929/30

The huge armfulls of bluebells held by Jean Juby and her cousin Henry Jones had just been gathered from Edgefield woods. Mr George Jones, Henry's father, farmed at Edgefield at this time, but later moved to Burgh Hall Farm at Melton Constable.

THE GROCERY STORE, WEST END, BRISTON – *c.* **1895**

The owner, Mr Samuel Reynolds, stands on the right, outside his recently-built shop. By 1900, Mrs Augusta Reynolds is listed as the proprietor. In later years it passed to their son Sidney, who had a Hardware Store – a wooden building, further down the Edgefield Road. Mr Reynolds was also a cycle agent with premises in Church Street, part of Waterloo House, which in turn passed to his son also named Sidney. The family also owned the shop opposite the church, occupied by Mr Ernie Riches the hairdresser.

GROCERY STORE, WEST END, BRISTON – 1935

The same shop as on the previous page, only now forty-five years on. It is Samuel's son, Sidney, who was a little boy on that picture and is now the proprietor of this store. He is seen here, with his two grandchildren Granville and Yvonne Eke, with flags decorating the shop for the 1935 Jubilee celebrations.

MR AND MRS E C WHITTRED, WEST END, BRISTON

Mr Ernie Whittred is seen here with his wife in their greenhouse in the early days of their marriage. He was Secretary of the Oddfellows' Hall (Manchester Unity) now demolished. He also ran the Cinema there two nights per week, on Thursdays and Fridays, with the projector coming from Holt Cinema by car for the film shows. Mr Whittred could be seen writing at his desk, with the sash window wide open in the summertime, and he would have a word with anyone who happened to be passing. The house where he lived stands facing the end of Edgefield Road.

HARVESTING AT FROGMORE FARM – *c.* 1927

Gathering the harvest are Alfred Williamson the farmer, assisted by Billy 'Sixer' on the cart – so called as he was of very small stature, and two other un-named helpers. Frogmore Farm House is seen in the background. The mules were ex-war dept (WW1). They starred in the film The Private Life of Don Juan.

AND FINALLY, HUNWORTH VILLAGE – Late 1930s

Hunworth is a tiny village in a valley between two hills. The road at the bottom front of picture is from Briston. It continues on up a steeper hill towards Holt, known as Hunney Hill. The little shop on the green was a General Store kept by Mr Kendle. The door was similar to a stable door, it opened in two halves. At the bottom of the hill off picture to the left was a farm kept in those days by Mr Andrews. Sadly, the little shop is no more, closed like so many other little village shops, so essential to village life in the past – they call it 'progress'.

Picture courtesy: Peter Jackson.

Acknowledgements

My grateful thanks are due to the following:

Dick and Molly Barwick for pages 88, 93 and 95.

Mr C M Blake for pages 57 and 58.

Mr John Carter for pages 14 and 62.

Mr R Casserley for permission to use his late father's photographs, pages 37 and 40.

Mr and Mrs Gaskins for information on Churchmans pages 18 and 19.

Mr Peter Jackson for valuable information and many photographs.

Mrs Sybil Kirk for information from her letters which I kept from Book One.

Mr David Lowe for the picture on page 9.

Mrs Rene Mendham for pictures on pages 63 and 64.

Mr and Mrs Michael Rutland for the page 7 photo, and pages 60 and 66.

Mr Philip Standley for postcard on page 15.

Mrs Jean Tufts for naming names and pictures on pages 72 and 105.

Mrs Ann West for picture on page 99.

Miss Anna Williamson for page 83.

And not forgetting my daughter Chrissie, for photocopying, typing and all her patience in correcting my mistakes.

Grateful thanks are also due to John Nickalls for making this book possible and to Ashley Gray for his assistance.

Local Titles
Published by John Nickalls Publications

A GARLAND OF WAVENEY TALES
A compilation of illustrated tales from Suffolk
of yesteryear

A LEVEL COUNTRY
Sketches of its Fenland folk and history

A PHARMACIST'S TALE
The joys, delights and disappointments encountered
preserving pharmacy history

CURIOUSITIES OF NORFOLK
A county guide to the unusual

GREAT OUSE COUNTRY
Sketches of its riverside folk and history
from source to mouth

MELTON CONSTABLE, BRISTON & DISTRICT – BOOK ONE
A portrait in old picture postcards

MELTON CONSTABLE, BRISTON & DISTRICT – BOOK TWO
A further portrait in old picture postcards

NATURE TRAILS IN NORTHAMPTONSHIRE

NEWMARKET, TOWN AND TURF
A pictorial tour

NORTH NORFOLK
A portrait in old picture postcards

NORWICH – THEN AND NOW
A look at the city through old postcards and modern
photographs

IN AND AROUND NORWICH – THEN AND NOW
A further look at Norwich and district

NORWICH – THEN AND NOW
A third selection of old picture postcards

ROBBER BARONS AND FIGHTING BISHOPS
The Norman influence in East Anglia

SHIRES, SALES AND PIGS
The story of an Ely family of Auctioneers.
George Comins, 1856–1997

SUFFOLK'S LIFEBOATS
A portrait in postcards and photographs

S'WONDERFUL
A symphony of musical memories

'SMARVELLOUS
More musical memories